Manipulation And Persuasion

An Effective Guide On How To Spot Covert Emotional Manipulation, Detect Deception And Defend Yourself From Persuasion Techniques And Toxic People

Written By

Richard Neel

Table of Contents

INTRODUCTION

Thank you for purchasing this book!

The founders continue to identify modeling as the core of the field. However, its essence is disputed; for example, Bostic St Clair & Grinder emphasizes a nonverbal approach, which avoids active thought or interpretation and contrasts with the more analytical focus of Dilts. The NLP modeling inspired specifically a contemporary European scientific approach, known as "Psychophenomenology" (Vermersch 2004).

The frequently asked question about NLP is that it has a definition. As mentioned above, writers emphasize pragmatism in the field and seldom display interest in the articulation of NLP as a theory. Because NLP has also aimed at modeling what works, proof of diverse methods can be found in NLP interventions focused (including) on cognitive/compartmental strategies, gestalt care, hypnotherapy, family therapy, and short care. Tosey and Mathison for further discussion of NLP learning theory (2003; 2008).

The NLP has epistemological concepts underlying the mechanisms by which people interpret, observe, and learn, as stated by Dilts and DeLozier. Usually formulated for practitioners as a series of 'presumptions' (Dilts & DeLozier 2000), these seem to be focused primarily on the ecological and cybernetic concern of Gregory Bateson. NLP thus applies itself to a cybernetic understanding of the structure and function of awareness and conceptualization processes.

Neuro-Linguistic Programming In Learning

Neurological programming is common in the field of personal development and self-motivation, and its teaching and learning value is also recognized. Two methods in neuro-linguistic programming,

spatial orientation, and presupposition, are known to be very consistent with Howard Gardner's theory on multiple intelligences. Perceptional perception is the ability to see something from another's viewpoint, a way of better comprehension. This method can be used in discussions, interviews, and the development of healthy limits and self-conception. It encourages 'putting yourself in the shoes of others' and can also be used to assist with bullying and behavioral issues. The presumption involves unspoken meanings in speech. For example, if a teacher offers the student the option between a questionnaire now and completing the lecture first, the message that all tasks must be completed is obvious, but it is not expressed clearly so. The opportunity to make a choice helps the learner to concentrate on their decision rather than to question the guidance of the instructor.

A paper presented at the European Conference on Educational Research provides a debate on how teaching and learning should use the neuro language programming approach. The following are among the many comparisons between teaching and neuro-linguistic programming:

In a collaborative teacher-learner relationship, reciprocal feedback helps to create meaning.

Every contact can have an effect on learning. Language and actions of teachers affect students at a minimum of two levels: their understanding of the topic in question and their confidence in the environment, including learning.

Awareness of teachers' actions, use of words, and how sensitive they are to the effects of these words and behavior on learners are vital to the success of teaching and learning processes.

According to this good article on the British Council website, the neuro-linguistic training is intended to aid in the fluency of languages, because teaching nonverbal communication in combination with phonology and functional language yields better results.

Enjoy your reading!

The Internet and Dark Psychology

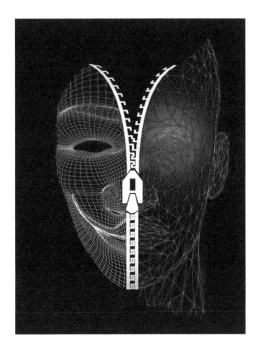

It is a fact that psychology is a scientific study that encompasses the study of human thoughts, behavior, emotions, mind, and so on. The beautiful thing is when one gets a deeper understanding

of how psychology operates; it can significantly benefit oneself and our everyday interactions with others. Man is a social being; therefore, it must process social behaviors that psychology seeks to understand, most time explains and sometimes predicts.

Despite having many branches, a large part of psychology aims to diagnose and treat mentally derailed individuals who possess a threat to the general public. Depending on the perspective, Psychologists are versatile and cuts across many other areas.

Also, note that psychology is all around you, your everyday activity, and your interaction with others, that TV commercial you saw recently, the print ads, the website you are most frequent on, and so on. All of these are either trying to persuade or convince you to bulge to whatever they are trying to offer.

Interestingly, there is psychology for any human problem, no matter the age or gender, which is why a psychologist is bent on making life better and improving human behavior. As constructive, educative, and informative as psychology, maybe, there is a dark side.

This aspect focuses on human consciousness as it relates to people's nature on or victimizing others.

Dark psychology aims to understand the various thoughts, reasoning, perception, or feelings that often lead to human predatory behavior because it entails the inhumane and brutal victimization of others

without any reasonable human comprehension. Predators commit theft, abuse, and violence upon their victims, and they appear in any form of personality. They are most times less compassionate and suspicious-looking.

Trolls generally can be annoying and irritating and can also be an agent of destruction/destruction. An internet troll starts quarrel and offends people on the internet. According to psychology, such people sometimes might have dark personality traits to them. They live such a life based on their sadistic nature, and others must suffer the same fate, and they naturally make you feel bad. Most times, there is a psychological disorder triggered by experience or an ongoing occurrence. When you encounter one, the best thing to do is completely ignoring them as they feed on your suffering, which gives them great pleasure. These internet trolls can be called a predator. These people are first-class cyberbullies, stalkers, criminals, sexual predators, and the likes. These people use the power of the internet to gather useful information about their victims or targets.

A predator can be a group of people or persons that one way or the other, directly or indirectly, enjoys stalking, exploring, and victimizing unsuspecting individuals by using the power of information communication technology (ICT). They are often consumed with their desire for power, imaginable fantasies, or just suffering from loneliness and searching for acceptance. Age or gender is not a barrier as a predator can be of any age, gender, or economic status. Initially, all we had was the human predator. Still, with the rise of the technology age, things are now even more complicated as predators harness ICT's power and use it to their advantage, create profiles, and stay almost untraceable.

Dark Traits and Online Activities

The internet is a world on its own. It is a chain of network communicating with other billion systems out there as long as you are connected and the other party also, no matter where you are, you

would be connected. You have access to almost anything you can think of. Once you stay connected and made communication way easier, information is just a click away. Despite having wonderful advantages, the disadvantages are life-threatening. One of the common disadvantages is that people work online 24/7 and spend a lot of time sitting while working in front of a computer often get ill. They get weaker, develop eye issues, back pain, and the likes. Some people get addicted, some fall into depression and isolation, and other serious health issues, while many end up with serious social issues or psychological disorders.

The internet often encourages the use of different behaviors and activities offline to be practical zed online. Imagine someone addicted to sex, games, or shopping. When such a person gets online, it becomes unlimited, which later turns into a habit. If, as a normal being, the internet has such an effect, imagine what it would pose in the hands of a predator. Narcissism is proud and lacks empathy. Machiavellianism is manipulative and lacks morals, while psychopathy is selfish and remorseless. Above all, traits, according to research, have some things in common such as the lack of empathy.

Categorically, the dark personality triad is a big influence in the behaviors of predators that trolls online. The online behavior of a Psychopathy can be remorseless while a Machiavellianism manipulates, and Narcissism preoccupied with getting attention because of their self-behavior. With all of these traits, one can easily pinpoint an internet troll that possesses a dark personality. Several researchers discovered that personality triad behaviors are mostly found on social media platforms like Facebook. Unlike the Narcissist, most trolls have a psychopathic tendency who promotes themselves or social status by the same social media platform.

Since he has pride, the online activity would be a display of superiority by uploading images that shouts expensive. They can be materialistic and display a sense of superiority; they can be domineering and a thirst for power and status. Machiavellianism, on the other hand, even

though they can have self-interest, but theirs is to manipulate and deceive unknowing victims to achieve their own goals. The Psychopath, in their way, is the destructive one of all the three personalities.

The Psychopath has no conscience, is violent, and very aggressive. Psychopathy is attracted to people who catch their attention either by social life or social status. Hypothetically speaking, Psychopathic is most likely associated with trolling and are more attracted to popular people on Facebook. On the other hand, Narcissism might not be a troll but see themselves as superior to everyone. They look down on people, and they believe that they are special. Above all, Psychopathic traits can be sadistic and may find pleasure in harming others for fun's sake because they derive pleasure from it. So, it is acceptable to say that abnormal online behavior is mostly psychopathic traits.

How the Internet Promotes Different Vices and Negative Traits

The majority doesn't know that the internet is like an onion bulb consisting of different layers; we have the surface, which is accessible to everyone, like your Google or Yahoo, where we can buy things online or access our social media handles and the likes. Surprisingly, this surface web does not even make up for 10% of the internet we use. The remaining 90% is the real deal. They are what we call Deep Web and Dark net, respectively. The deep web is only accessible to authorized persons as this is where private data such as legal documentation belonging to the government are stored. Also, medicals and academic information and not left out. Authorized and special services oversee the Deep Web.

Moving deeper is the Dark net, which is the most dangerous of them all; it uses the Onion Router (TOR). To have access, one would have to download the app. With just a click, one can end up in dangerous sites like the uncensored hidden wiki and many more.

A site such as these provides information on drugs, weapons, pornography, and so on. Various transactions can take place on the Dark net using our everyday services, such as FedEx. A significant thing to note is that the Dark net users can be anonymous; every personal data can be concealed, secure, and untraceable.

Psychologists have understood that there is a big relationship between dark personality traits, the human mind, and the internet's dark side. Some researchers even claimed that the amount of time spent online could increase or lead people to develop dark traits.

The question now is it the various online activities that attract individuals who already exhibit a good percentage of dark personality traits? Or can we say it is a long period spent on the internet that has increased these individuals' traits? There is a probability that both assumptions might be correct either way. The internet has, over time, become a sort for humans to explore their dark side. The internet has bred addicts because some negative traits seem to have been nurtured and encouraged by the internet, which now possesses negative consequences when offline. The internet's negative effect on personality is a functional part of online Psychology. With the help of the internet-related digital lifestyle, its effect on gambling or shopping is clear evidence of impulse control disorder.

Another negative trait is the rise of suicidal persons; it is no news that the suicide rate has risen over the years. One cannot commit suicide online, but the increase in suicide definitely can be linked to an internet effect. The internet has also promoted online shaming, cyber bullying, name-calling, and so on, which is regarded as a violent online discourse that can lead to a less cohesive offline society.

Covert Emotional Manipulation

Covert emotional manipulation is used by people who want to gain power or control over you by deploying deceptive and underhanded tactics. Such people want to change the way you

think and behave without realizing what they are doing. In other words, they use techniques that can alter your perceptions in such a way that you think that you are doing it out of your own free will. Covert emotional manipulation is "covert" because it works without you being consciously aware of that fact. People who are good at deploying such techniques can get you to do their bidding without your knowledge; they can hold you psychologically captive.

Covert emotional manipulation is more common than you might think. Since it's subtle, people are rarely aware that it's happening to them, and in some cases, they may never even notice. Only keen outside observers may be able to tell when this form of manipulation is going on.

You might know someone who used to be fun and friendly, then she got into a relationship with someone else, and a few years down the line, she seems to have a completely different personality. If it's an old friend, you might not even recognize the person she has become. That is how powerful covert emotional manipulation can be. It can completely overhaul someone's personality without them even realizing it. The manipulator will chip away at you little by little, and you will accept minute changes that fly under the radar until the old you are replaced by a different version of you, build to be subservient to the manipulator.

Covert emotional manipulation works like a slow-moving coup. It requires you to make small progressive concessions to the person that is trying to manipulate you. In other words, you let go of tiny aspects of your identity to accommodate the manipulative person, so it never registers in your mind that there is something bigger at play.

When the manipulative person pushes you to change in small ways, you will comply because you don't want to sweat the small stuff. However, there is a domino effect that occurs as you start conceding to the manipulative person. You will be more comfortable making subsequent concessions, and your personality will be erased and replaced in a cumulative progression.

Covert emotional manipulation occurs to some extent in all social dynamics. Look at how it plays out in romantic relationships, in friendships, and at work.

Emotional manipulation in relationships

There are many emotional manipulations in romantic relationships, and it's not always malicious. For example, women try to modify men's behavior to make them more "housebroken"; that is just normal. However, certain instances of manipulation where the person's intention is malicious, and he/she is motivated by a need to control or dominate over the other person.

Positive reinforcement is perhaps the most used covert manipulation technique in romantic relationships. Your partner can get you to do what he wants by praising you, flattering you, giving you attention, offering your gifts, and acting affectionately.

Even the seemingly nice things in relationships can turn out to be covert manipulation tools and props. For instance, your girlfriend could use intense sex as a weapon to reinforce a certain kind of behavior in you. Similarly, men can use charm, appreciation, or gifts to reinforce certain behaviors in the women they are dating.

Some sophisticated manipulators use what psychologists call intermittent positive reinforcement to gain control over their partners. They will shower the victim with intense positive reinforcement for a certain period and then switch to just giving her normal attention and appreciation levels. After a random interval of time, he will again go back to the intense positive reinforcement. When the victim gets used to the special treatment, it's taken away, and when she gets used to normal treatment, the special treatment is brought back, and it all seems arbitrary. Now, the victim will get to a place where she becomes sort of "addicted" to the special treatment, but she has no idea how to get it, so she starts doing whatever the perpetrator wants in the hope that one of the things she does will bring back the intense positive reinforcement. In other words, she effectively becomes subservient to the perpetrator.

Negative reinforcement techniques are also used in relationships to manipulate others covertly. For example, partners can withhold sex to compelling the other person to modify their behavior in a specific way. People also use techniques such as the silent treatment and withholding of love and affection.

Some malicious people can create a false sense of intimacy by pretending to open up to you. They could share personal stories and talk about their hopes and fears. When they do this, they create the impression that they trust you, but their intention may be to get you to feel a sense of obligation towards them.

Manipulators also use well-calculated insinuations to get you to react in a certain way at the moment to modify your behavior in the long run. People in relationships are always trying to figure out what the other person wants out of that relationship. A manipulative person can drop hints to get you to do what they want without having responsibility for your actions because they can always argue that you misinterpreted what they meant.

Dropping hints isn't always malicious (for example, if your girlfriend wants you to propose, she may leave bridal magazines out on the table). However, malicious insinuations can be very hurtful, and they can chip away at your self-esteem. Your partner can suggest you are gaining weight, and you aren't making enough money or suggesting that your cooking skills aren't any good. People use insinuations to get away with "saying without saying," any number of hurtful things that could affect your self-esteem. Emotional manipulations in friendships

Covert emotional manipulation is quite common in friendships and casual relationships. Friendships tend to progress slower than romantic relationships, but that means that it can take a lot more time for you to figure out if your friends are manipulative. Manipulation in friendships can be confusing because even well-meaning friends can come across as malicious. That's because there is a certain social rivalry between even the closest friends, which explains the concept of "ferneries."

Manipulative friends tend to be passive-aggressive. This is where they manipulate you into doing what they want by involving mutual friends rather than directly coming to you. Passive aggression works as a manipulation technique because it denies you a chance of directly addressing whatever issue your friend is raising. So, in a manner of speaking, you lose by default.

For example, if a friend wants you to do her a favor, instead of coming out and asking you, she goes to a mutual friend and suggests that she asks you on her behalf. When a mutual friend approaches you, it becomes very difficult for you to turn down the request because of added social pressure. When you say no, your whole social circle now perceives you as selfish.

Passive aggression can also involve the use of silent treatment to get you to comply with a request. Imagine where one of your friends talks to everyone else but you. It's going to be incredibly awkward for you, and everyone will start prying, wondering what the problem is between the two of you, and taking sides on the matter.

Friends can also covertly manipulate you by using subtle insults. They can give you back-handed compliments that have hidden meanings. What they meant by the compliment, you will realize that it's an insult in disguise, which will bruise your self-esteem and possibly modify your behavior.

Some friends can manipulate you by going on a "power trip" and controlling your social interactions. For example, there are those friends who insist that every time you hang out, it should be in their apartment or at a social venue of their choosing. Such friends often intend to dominate your friendship, so they are keen to always have the "home ground advantage" over you. They'll try to push you out of your comfort zone just so that you can reveal your weaknesses, and you can then become more emotionally reliant on them.

Manipulative friends tend to excessively capitalize on your friendship, and to a disproportionate degree. They will ask you for lots of favors with no regard for your time or your effort. They are the friends who will leverage your friendship every time they need something but then make excuses when it's their turn to reciprocate.

Emotional manipulation at work

There are some reasons why your colleague may want to manipulate you. It could be you are on the same career path, so he wants to make you look bad. It could be that he is lazy, and he wants to stick you with his responsibilities. It could also be that he is a sadist, and he wants to see you suffer.

One-way people at work exert their dominance over others is by stressing them out and then, almost immediately, relieving the stress. Say, for example, you make a minor error on a report, and your boss calls you into his office. He makes a big fuss and threatens to fire you, but then towards the end, he switches gears and reassures you that your job is secure as long as you do what he wants. That kind of

manipulation works on people because it makes them afraid and gives them a sense of obligation at the same time.

Some colleagues can manipulate you by doing you small favors and then reminding you of those favors every time they want something from you. For instance, if you made an error at work and a colleague covered for you, he may hold it over your head for months or even years to come, and he is going to guilt you into feeling indebted to him.

Colleagues can also manipulate you by leaving you out of the loop when passing across important information. The intention here is to get you to mess up so that they can better stand with the boss or with other colleagues. When you discover that someone is leaving you out of the loop at work and you confront them, they could feign innocence and pretend that it was a genuine mistake on their part, or they could find a way to turn it around and blame you.

People with dark personality traits tend to be hyper-competitive at work, and they won't hesitate to use underhanded means to pull one over you. Most colleagues turn out to be good friends, but you should be careful with colleagues that are overly eager to befriend you. It could be that they want to learn more about you so that they can figure out your strengths and weaknesses and find ways to use them against you. Narcissists, Machiavellians, and psychopaths are very good at scheming at work, so don't let them catch you off guard.

Types of Emotional Manipulation

Playing the Victim

This is a manipulation technique where the manipulator casts himself or herself as a victim to avoid taking responsibility for whatever has gone wrong in his or her life. When a manipulator plays the victim, he willfully ignores the logical view that he is responsible for his actions. Either way, if you are the target of their manipulation, they'll most certainly find a way of making you take responsibility for them.

The purpose of playing the victim is to avoid responsibility and gain others' sympathy. People who use this technique want the other person to see them as wounded people who are suffering in one way or another, elicit empathy, and reap the benefits of that sympathy.

Manipulators may play the victim to create a cloud that conceals their true identity as the aggressive in a relationship, especially in public. For example, manipulators who abuse their private partners will pretend to be the actual victims when the couples are in public, with family members, or with mutual friends. This way, the abusive manipulator manages his public impression, which gives him more power over his victim.

These manipulators often choose kind-hearted people as their victims because they know that they don't like to see others suffer. Kind- hearted people also hate to think that they are the source of other people's suffering. If the manipulators imply that their suffering resulted from their actions, they will go out of their way to rectify the situation.

This manipulation technique is often invoked by manipulators when they are confronted about their behavior. For example, if you have such a person in your life (e.g., a family member or a partner) and call him out for living leeching off you instead of finding a job, he will immediately take the victim's stance to throw a bunch of excuses at you.

Seduction

Seduction is an integral part of courtship, and everyone uses it at some point in their lives. When used for manipulation purposes, seduction is defined as "using one's attractiveness and a myriad of romantic techniques (including the promise of sex, or actual sex) to advantage of others or to gain control over them."

Seducers manipulate their victims by playing on their need to feel valued. We all have an innate need to be desired by others, feel valued and appreciated, and be liked. That's why the vast majority of people are susceptible to seduction techniques. When a seducer gives you attention, it makes you feel special, and you may end up allowing them to gain control over a certain aspect of your life. We naturally tend to be obsessed with ourselves. When someone compliments us, we never really think it's about them wanting something from us.

Seduction is an effective manipulation technique partly because, as a society, we are more focused on positive psychology (teaching people how to feel good about themselves), and we rarely on the reality that people are malicious, and we need to guard against their machinations.

Being a Powerful Dependent

These are manipulators who hide behind the mask of weakness so that they can control other people. They will pretend to be powerless or helpless, and once they have you doing their bidding, they dominate over you and making it seem that your life's mission is to please them and to avoid letting them down.

You can tell a powerful dependent if you have someone in your life who has difficulty making any necessary decision (or taking any meaningful action) without seeking assurance or advice from you. As long as you are around them, these people will not act; they'll wait for you to do everything for them. They are often afraid of taking chances and failing, so they'll let you do everything that involves any level of risk so that in case it turns out badly, they can claim it's your fault.

Powerful dependents tend to experience anxiety and distress when they are left alone. They always need to be with someone, so they'll aggressively pursue relationships with their targets. Early in the relationship, they'll start showing signs of dependency by letting you make all the important decisions (including scheduling all your dates and figuring out all your plans).

Triangulation

Triangulation is a manipulation technique that involves piling social pressure on someone to dominate them or control them. When a manipulator uses triangulation against you, he or she will try to recruit other people to help them to compel you to do certain things for the manipulator.

There are several different iterations of the triangulation technique. The first and most common one involves the manipulator asking someone else to ask you for a favor on his or her behalf. For example, is when a friend wants to borrow money from you, he may ask another friend (possibly one that you are closer to) to ask you on his behalf. When this happens, it becomes tough for you to say "No" because you feel more pressured to appear generous.

In marriages or other family dynamics, manipulators can modify this technique by using a child or another family member as a messenger to make it a lot harder for you to turn them down.

The triangulation technique works when a manipulative person tells his or her partner that a mutual friend was trying to seduce him or her.

In this case, the triangulation technique serves two purposes; first, it drives a wedge between the target and the mutual friend. Second, it creates a sense of jealousy and insecurity in the target so that they become more inclined to do what the manipulator wants (to salvage the relationship).

Deliberate Misinterpretation

Deliberate misinterpretation refers to several manipulation techniques where the manipulator intentionally twists your words. It's either to make you look bad or to make themselves look good. They willfully opt to misunderstand you so that they can claim to be hurt by your words or so that they can get you to take certain actions to make up for a mistake they know you haven't committed.

These kinds of manipulators twist your words as a way of deflecting from the real issue at hand. They know that if you have a rational adult conversation, they won't come off looking good, so they deliberately misunderstand the point you are making to force you to go on the defensive.

Use of Emotional Outbursts

In this technique, manipulators use emotional outbursts to get what they want. In most cases, these outbursts involve negative emotions (e.g., angry yelling, crying, etc.), and in most cases, the aim is to keep you from asking certain questions that you may have at the moment.

Outbursts (especially those that involve anger) are considered by most psychologists to be the adult versions of tantrums. Outbursts, as adults, never learned to process their emotions when they were younger.

Manipulators who use this technique often do it in the presence of an audience because they know that it makes the whole situation more awkward for the target. Often, they'll target an introverted victim, so they are very uncomfortable about being in the spotlight. If the

manipulator wants to ask the victim for something, they will wait until they are in the presence of other people, and they bring up the topic. If the victim tries to be reasonable, the manipulator will keep raising their voice until everyone is staring at them. The victim may immediately cave in out of embarrassment.

Projecting onto Others

Projectors are manipulators who work off the premise that they are perfect. Others are inherently flawed, so whatever does wrong in a relationship is always the other person's fault. A projector will assign you all of his negative characteristics and traits. If you are a perfectly reasonable person, sometimes you might even think that he is doing it as a joke, but he is usually dead serious about it.

Projectors tend to be narcissists; they have very high entitlement levels, and they believe that they can do no wrong. There has to be an alternative explanation for their shortcomings, so they have to find someone on whom to project those shortcomings.

Intimidation and Bullying

As a manipulation technique, intimidation comes in two forms; covert and overt. Both forms of manipulation are particularly effective when the person using them has the ability to articulate emotional tenacity by convincing the target that he has the resolve to cause serious harm (either physical or emotional) to him. Intimidators have perfected the art of convincing people that they are no match to them if the dispute they are having comes down to a battle of wills.

Intimidation is about forcing the target to go on the defensive so that they cannot hold the manipulator accountable for something that he may have done. It may also be about instilling fear in the target so that they feel that there is no choice but to give the manipulator what he wants.

Intimidation can sometimes involve the use of several manipulation tactics at once; the manipulator fires off emotional attacks from several angles so that the target finds himself in a position where he has no choice but to comply.

One-Upmanship

One-upmanship refers to a manipulation technique that involves using criticisms, snide remarks, self-praise, and other verbal techniques to show that the manipulator is superior to the person on the receiving end of his attacks. It is to make the target feel inferior and to establish the manipulator's dominance over him. The manipulator wants to be seen by the target and third parties as the smart one in that dynamic.

The point is to make your accomplishments and your problems seem minuscule compared to his. When you are in our relationship with such a person, you are unlikely to receive any emotional support.

Guilt-Tripping

Guilt-tripping is an emotional manipulation technique that involves making someone feel guilty or responsible for something so that you can oblige them to atone for it by performing certain favors for you.

Manipulators guilt-trip their targets by finding real or perceived transgressions, bringing them up, exaggerating the impacts that the transgressions have had on them, explaining that the targets need to make things right, and then suggesting ways for the targets to make it right.

Guilt-tripping is a passive-aggressive manipulation technique, and it mostly works in interpersonal dynamics where the target is emotionally invested in the welfare of the manipulator.

Manipulators often try to make the guilt proportional to what they want from the target, so if they want something major, they may pile one several perceived transgressions to force the target to bear a larger guilt burden.

For a guilt-trip to work, the target doesn't necessarily need to have any real transgressions on his plate; sometimes, victims can be guilt-tripped by merely using the sense of obligated they feel towards the manipulator. For example, the manipulator may say something like, "if you loved me, you would do this for me." The target will then feel guilty, and he will do what the manipulator wants to assuage that guilt.

How to Read and Analyze People

The first part of being able to influence and manipulate someone will be when you learn how to read them. You have to get a good analysis of the other person, or you will end up

with a lot of trouble in the process trying to get them to do what you want or wasting time with a strategy that doesn't work for that particular target.

The good news is that there are quite a few steps that you can take to figure out who someone is so that you can learn more about them and pick out the right manipulation technique to get what you want.

Learning the baseline of the target

You need to learn how to get a baseline on the target we wish to work with. The baseline is just going to be when we notice how the person behaves when they are not stressed out, overly happy, or have any other reason to act in a different way than what is normal.

While it is common to learn how to watch out for body language to help us know if the other person likes us or lying or not, you will find that not everyone will behave in the same manner under those circumstances. When you can take some time to learn the baseline of the target, you will learn how they will behave regularly, and then it is easier to catch when there are changes to that behavior.

Learn the different personality types

Every person you encounter will be a little bit different from the others, and this is fine. Learning who they are and why they react to

things in a certain way will be hard to get each time because all of us are created to be unique and special.

Several personality types are recognized at large, and we all will lean closer to one of them or one combination of them than the other. You can use these different types of personalities, and the things that come with them, to help you get a little bit better feel of the target you are trying to analyze.

Learn the different personality types

First, we have the analysts. These will be the people who like to study things and are going to rely a lot on the facts presented to them. They have emotions, but they are not going to base any decisions they make on these emotions. Do not waste your time with emotional tactics to get them to do what you want. Instead, if you can get them many facts about why they should react one way over another, you are more likely to get the results you want.

Following on the list is going to be the diplomat. These are the people who can think things through in a manner that is going to benefit other people and not just themselves. They use logic, but there is often a bit of emotion in the mix. If you want to manipulate this kind of person, you have to be ready to add in some facts coupled with emotion and more. They are an interesting group to work with, and you will find that reading them will give you a lot of the good practice you are looking for.

And the final group of people we will take a look at is known as the explorers. These people will have a knack for being creative, trying something new, and seeing where life takes them.

Read between the lines.

Reading between the lines, which can also be seen as interpreting some of the hidden meanings of what others are trying to tell you, is absolutely a skill you can learn. While you may miss out on some

things that the other person is telling you, you can likely figure out a lot of what they are saying if you pay more attention. You need to take steps to read between the lines and catch on to the true meaning of what someone is trying to tell you.

You need to learn how to listen carefully. Do not spend more time figuring out how to respond to the other person than you do listening to them. You need to nod and smile to show them that you are paying attention. Use some neutral statements to help keep the other person talking and sharing with you, and then rephrase what they have told you to ensure that you understood it properly. This will help you to get the best results when you are trying to analyze them.

The basics of body language

Body language will be something that you need to pay attention to when it comes to the other person you want to target. It is going to open up a lot of doors to you about whether they feel comfortable or start to suspect something, how far you can push them, and whether you are going to make some progress with them or not. And there are so many different things that you need to focus on when it comes to body language that it is definitely in your best interest to learn about it as quickly as possible. There are so many different parts of body language that you can focus on, and this can help you get a different outlook on what the person is trying to say to you. For example, if someone is constantly sighing, checking their watches, and looking towards the door, you already know that they are not interested in the conversation that the two of you are having and want to end it.

Thought patterns

You will find that you can read other people's thoughts and actions, as long as you are willing to take some time to do it.

There are going to be several types of people. We will split them up into four groups, but most people are some combination of two different ones out of these four. You will find that learning which one you are targeting will make a world of difference in how well you understand them and how much you will be able to manipulate them.

The four personality types that will include the thought patterns that you have will include extrovert vs. introvert and logical vs. empathy. These can go together, such as being an extroverted empathy or an introverted, logical person. Still, they will have different personalities that make them stick out from the rest.

Extrovert.

This kind of person is going to be the life of the party. They find that they can recharge their batteries and feel so much better at any time that they can get out or socialize. They prefer large groups of people to talk with and share stories with, but any socialization will help them feel so much better. They have a lot of friends, regardless of whether it is required for their job or not.

Introvert.

There is often a misunderstanding that these individuals don't like others. They like others, but in smaller doses than the extrovert. The introvert likes other people but finds that when they socialize, their energy will be drained out, and they need to have some time to be alone and recharge before they start to socialize with others again. They often stick with just a few close friends and will usually not have a lot of contacts that they work with unless it is required by their job to do so.

Logical kind of person.

This person may be an extrovert or an introvert, but they will spend a lot of time focusing on facts and statistics compared to other people. They want you to show them why one thing is a better idea than the other. If you can show a lot of proof that this product is the best because of the studies done on it or many numbers for other reasons, you will find that it is easier to manipulate others to do what you want.

Empathy.

It isn't that these people don't think through their decisions, but they feel their emotions so well that it is easy for them to fall prey to others who need help or pull on the emotions a little bit. Empathy knows how it feels to suffer and wants to do what they can to help others out. When you want to sell something to them, you won't show them the facts and figures. You would show empathy about how the vehicle may help them to keep their family safe.

Analyzing the target, you want to work with when it comes to manipulation will take some time and effort. It is not something that happens in just a few seconds in most cases. Taking care of this analysis and learning what makes the other person behave in a certain manner or do certain things will make a world of difference.

Empaths and Their Vulnerabilities

An empath is a person who can share in other people's emotions as if those emotions were their own. If the darkness continuum were a scale, empaths would be on one end while

the dark triad personalities would be on the other. Empaths are often vulnerable targets for manipulation by the dark triad personalities, and it will be easy to see why as you read on. It is important to note that being an empathy is not the same as being empathetic. Being empathetic refers to having the capacity to understand the feelings and thoughts of other people. It is a crucial component of emotional intelligence that involves the willingness to put your judgments aside to experience things from another person's perspective.

Empaths have a heightened grasp on other people's mental and emotional states. Sometimes, they will perceive other people's emotional and mental energy states without being told. An empath may be able to sense the subtle energy signals given off by another person without necessarily having a conversation with said person on what may be taking place emotionally or mentally for that individual.

Empaths tend to be very nurturing. They are always seeking to heal those around them who seem to be in pain. For this reason, empaths make very easy targets for predators. The relationship between an empath and a narcissist, for instance, is very toxic. This is because an empath will continue to feed the narcissist's constant need for attention and admiration at their expenses. The narcissist is the consistent taker in the relationship while the empath does all the giving.

Qualities of an Empath That Make Them Vulnerable

The highly intuitive nature of an empath is a positive and powerful quality. The capability to read a room's energy just by walking into it can be harnessed to the empath's benefit. Unfortunately, in many situations, an empath tends to be the victim in the story.

This is especially so when they cannot switch off from their caregiving role or create strong, energetic boundaries. Empaths can easily become doormats for the dark triad personalities because their mental and emotional cores are set up.

Emotional Sponges

Many people tend to naturally gravitate towards empaths because of the healing energy that empaths emit. It is not uncommon for strangers to open up to empaths about their life stories and suffering. The openness and lack of judgment that empaths exude are major reasons why empaths can draw others out of their shells. The broken person can heal their emotional wounds and unload their mental burdens by sharing empathy.

The downside of this scenario is that empaths are left to carry a mental and emotional energetic load that is not theirs. In the case where an empath has not established healthy boundaries, it is possible to get overwhelmed. For this reason, empaths are often advised to learn how to protect their energy against exploitation.

Inability to Prioritize Themselves

Most empaths often put themselves last regarding self-healing. An empath is usually the kind of person who will give someone their shirt to stay dry and warm while they go without. If an empath is unaware of this important component of their personality, they may find themselves emotionally drained without understanding why.

An empathy that is not attuned to the causes of their emotional drain may resort to putting up walls in a bid to protect themselves. Such an empath may not realize that setting more stringent boundaries would be a better solution.

Inability to Identify Toxicity

An empath will make every excuse before they finally admit that the said person is an emotional vampire. An emotional or energy vampire is a person who thrives in stealing other people's emotional energy to compensate for their failures and shortcomings. Emotional vampires are often people who are struggling with an unfulfilled need or childhood trauma. Instead of meeting this need internally, emotional vampires look to other people to fill the voids in their lives.

When an empath and an emotional vampire meet, the empathy takes on the nurturing role of healer and protector. The empathy takes the emotional vampire under their wing and helps the emotional vampire to the best of their ability. If the vampire is abusive in one way or another, an empath will often choose to stay and heal the vampire until they are in a better place. The empath's inability to be dismissive of other people's suffering means that they try to look for a backstory to every individual. If involved with a narcissist, the empathy might try to rationalize the narcissist's behavior resulting from childhood trauma. They will therefore stay in the relationship, hoping to change the narcissist. The unfortunate side of this story is that some people are just toxic to toxicity's sake and have no intention of changing. The empath's ability to give second, third and even fourth chances to undeserving people ends up being their undoing.

Introversion

While an empath can be extroverted, a significant number of empaths tend to be introverted. Empaths are often overwhelmed by crowds due to the huge amounts of energy generated by these crowds. As such, empaths may prefer one-on-one contact because they can absorb

the other person's energy without getting frayed. Introversion, in itself, is not a bad thing. Unfortunately, when an emotional vampire sets their sights on an introverted empathy, it is easier to isolate them as they are already open to this isolation in the first place. For instance, narcissists love isolating their victims, and the empathy who does not like to be in crowds in the first place makes quite an easy target.

Difficulty Saying "No"

It is never easy to say "no," especially when the request comes from a dear person. Most people are afraid of the very powerful but rather useless emotion of guilt when saying "no." To an average person, the aftermath of saying no is often awkwardness, guilt, and resentment. To an empath, these feelings are magnified sometimes to the point where they become unbearable. As such, it is often easier for an empath to say "yes" to keep the peace. When involved with a malignant narcissist, an empath will often be guilt-tripped into saying yes to all the narcissist's demands. Narcissists are particularly keen on utilizing guilt- tripping tactics, the cold shoulder/silent treatment to get what they want, and an empath, given their caring and nurturing nature, is an easy target.

Empaths versus Highly Sensitive People

Even though the terms empathy and highly sensitive people are often used interchangeably, they do not refer to the same thing. Generally, empaths are classified one level under highly sensitive people (HSP), owing to their heightened sensitivity to their surroundings. One of the key differences between an empath and a highly sensitive person is the medium they use to detect their environment changes. Empaths rely on other people's energy, while highly sensitive people tend to be attuned to the sensory stimuli present in a situation. For instance, let's say an empath and a highly sensitive person walk into the same room. The empathy might sense the negative energy emanating from the upset people in the room, while the highly sensitive person may be overwhelmed by the room's sights and sounds. If a heated argument is

ongoing in the room, the empathy will be overloaded by the anger, disgust, and contempt characteristic of the room. At the same time, the HSP may experience a fraying of their nerves thanks to the argument's loudness.

An empathy, especially one who is empowered enough to understand their own emotions outside of other people's, will often experience fluctuating energy levels while pinpointing exactly why that is happening. On the other hand, a highly sensitive person may feel overwhelmed by the energy in a place without understanding why this is happening. In this aspect, an empath is more attuned to themselves and their surroundings than a highly sensitive person.

Highly sensitive people tend to be consumed by their feelings. They may project these feelings to other people and fail to understand why people do not seem to share these emotions. This is yet another significant difference between empaths and highly sensitive people — the empathy absorbs those around them, while the HSP projects their emotions onto other people. For this reason, an empath and an HSP may be caught up in a relationship characterized by great codependence.

The sensitive nature of empaths and highly sensitive people make them both sitting ducks for manipulation. Psychological manipulation often works best on highly emotional people. Emotions, more often than not, will win over logic. By utilizing an empath's greatest asset, which is their emotional capacity, a manipulator can often get an empath to do whatever they want without even realizing it. Of course, a manipulator's tactics will work best on disempowered empaths who have not yet learned to harness their empathic abilities and shield themselves. Empowered empaths are those who have learned to control their power to the extent where they can walk away from draining situations because they can identify emotional vampires from a mile away.

The dark triad personalities are much harder to manipulate since they are the manipulators themselves. You will have greater progress manipulating an empath on any day than a narcissist.

Mind Control Tactics

With a basic understanding of what mind control entails, you are then ready to move on to the tactics involved in mind control. These are particularly dangerous, especially in

conjunction with the steps to priming the target for mind control. They are far more susceptible to the rest of the priming and the techniques used.

Develop Trust

The first step to set up control over someone else's mind is to develop trust. You cannot mind control someone else without first creating the trust necessary for the rest of the steps to follow without detection. You can use mirroring and other body languages in conjunction with love bombing or other manipulation tactics to create an artificial relationship. Regardless of how you do it, you must make sure the person you seek to control trusts you.

Destroy the Old Personality

Once you have established the relationship sufficiently, it is time to move on to the next step. Here, you need to destroy the individual's old personality. You cannot create the pseudo-personality that is meant to be loaded up with thoughts and beliefs rather than those of the individual you have targeted.

To destroy the old personality, you must convince them that their old personality is flawed somehow. This is why someone with low self- esteem is so much easier to overtake than someone confident.

When you can convince someone that they are inherently broken, flawed, or weak, they are more likely to enter a stage of questioning and doubt in their own identity.

Debilitation

With the busy individual questioning who they are and what they want in life, you can then move on to the debilitation stage. While not strictly necessary, the person you are attempting to manipulate was already particularly malleable as an individual. When you debilitate your target, you make them far more susceptible to your manipulation and thoughts and feelings you wish to install. It can be done through several methods—sleep deprivation, abuse, poor diets, drugs, or even physical or sexual assault. Anything to weaken the person as a whole and enable them to be more easily controlled goes here.

Personality Insertion

Through many of the mind control tactics that will be listed below, you will understand exactly how you can insert the personality of what you want into the other person. Thought control, such as limiting of choices and repetition and reinforcement, could slowly impose your thoughts and beliefs into the other person, slowly becoming internalized until the other person believes them as well or thinks he or she believes them.

Testing Your Control

The other person should be within your control. The particular methodology you will use within each step depends on your specific target. You will need to ensure that the methods you choose to use match up with who you want to control and how you want them to behave. You can now test your control by trying to see emotional reactions or watching to make sure that you have thoroughly conditioned the person to go through with whatever it is you want

Methods of Mind Control Repetition and Reinforcement

Repetition and reinforcement utilize the idea that if you say something to someone enough, they will begin to internalize it. This is what many people use to utilize affirmations, and it works in the negative as well. Through this method, you can convince other people to behave in ways you never thought possible by inserting your thoughts into their minds and making them believe they were their own. This is perfect for inserting a pseudo-personality to replace the personality of the individual you are controlling.

Limiting Choices Available

Limiting choices is another way to insert thoughts—you can sway the direction someone is thinking by making them think that they must choose between an artificially created false dichotomy or limited selection. Think of how you can give a child the illusion of choice by providing them with a few choices that you approve of rather than letting them make the decision themselves. Such as asking whether the child wants carrots or broccoli with dinner instead of asking if the child wants veggies for dinner. You can do this with adults as well—by implying that there are only a few acceptable choices, the other person's thoughts are limited just enough to be acceptable to you, no matter which choice is made.

Sleep Deprivation

When you need to break someone down, sleep deprivation is the easiest way to do so. With as little as 21 hours being necessary before signs of impairment become apparent, you can make someone far more susceptible to manipulation through sleep deprivation. If you can keep someone awake long enough, you will be able to control them simply because they are already exhausted subsequently and ready to pass out.

They are not going to have the mental fortitude to defend themselves. Emotional Manipulation
Isolation

Isolation strips anyone around them that could potentially help them defend themselves from various forms of manipulation and mind control. When someone has a large circle of friends, family, and loved ones who understand them as a person, any subtle personality changes are far more likely to be noticed early on, calling everything into question. If you can isolate your target, you make it less likely that you will be caught in the process of attempting to manipulate them.

How To Change People's

Emotions Through NLP

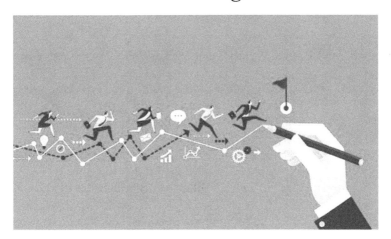

<u>How NLP Works</u>

If you are just coming across this topic for the first time, NLP may appear like magic or hypnosis. When a person is undergoing therapy, it digs deep into the unconscious mind of the patient and filters through different layers of beliefs. The person's approach or perception of life to deduce early childhood experiences are

responsible for a behavioral pattern.

In NLP, it is believed that everyone has the resources needed for positive changes in their own lives. The technique adopted here is meant to help in facilitating these changes.

Usually, when NLP is taught, it is done in a pyramidal structure. However, the most advanced techniques are left for those multi- thousand-dollar seminars. An attempt to explain this complicated subject is to state that the NLPer (as those who use NLP will often call themselves) is always paying keen attention to the person they are working on/with. Usually, the majority of NLPers are therapists and they are very likely to be well-meaning people. They achieved their aims by paying attention to those subtle cues like the movement of the eyes, flushing of the skin, dilation of the pupil, and subtle nervous tics. It is easy for an NLP user to quickly determine the following:

The side of the brain that a person predominantly uses.

The sense (smell, sight, etc.) that is more dominant in a person's brain.

The way the person's brain stores and makes use of information (the NLPer can deduce all this from the person's eye movement).

When they are telling a lie or concocting information.

When the NLP user has successfully gathered all this information, they begin to mimic the client in a slow and subtle manner by not only taking on their body language, but also by imitating their speech and mannerisms, so that they begin to talk with the language patterns that are aimed at targeting the primary senses of the client. They will typically fake the social cues that will easily make someone let their guard down so that they become very open and suggestible.

For example, when a person's sense of sight is their most dominant sense, the NLPer will use a language that is very laden with visual metaphors to speak with them. They will say things like: "do you see what I am talking about?" or "why not look at it this way?" For a person that has a more dominant sense of hearing, he will be approached with an auditory language like: "listen to me" or "I can hear where you're coming from."

To create a rapport, the NLPer mirrors the body language and the linguistic patterns of the other person. This rapport is a mental and physiological state which a human being gets into when they lose guard of their social senses. It is done when they begin to feel like the other person who they are conversing with is just like them.

Once the NLPer has achieved this rapport, they will take charge of the interaction by leading it in a mild and subtle manner. Thanks to the fact that they have already mirrored the other person, they will now begin to make some subtle changes in order to gain a certain influence on the behavior of the person. This is also combined with some similar subtle language patterns which lead to questions and a whole phase of some other techniques.

At this point, the NLPer will be able to tweak and twist the person to whichever direction they so desire. This only happens if the other person can't deduce that there is something going on because they assume everything that is occurring is happening organically or that they have given consent to everything.

What this means is that it is quite hard to make use of NLP to get other people to act out of character, but it can be used to get a person to give responses within their normal range of character.

At this point, what the NLP user seeks to do may be to either elicit or anchor. When they are eliciting, they make use of both leading and language to get the person to an emotional state of say, sadness. Once they can elicit this state, they can then lead it on with a physical cue by touching the other person's shoulder for example.

According to theory, whenever the NLP user touches the person's shoulder in the same manner, the same emotional state will resurface if they do it again. However, this is only made possible by the successful conditioning of the other person.

When undergoing NLP therapy, it is very possible for the therapist to adopt a content-free approach, which means the therapist can work effectively without taking a critical look at the problem or without even knowing about the problem at all. This means that there is room for privacy for the client as the therapist does not really need to be told about whichever event took place or whatever issue happened in the past.

Also, prior to the commencement of the therapy, there is an agreement that ensures that the therapist cannot disclose any information that means the interaction between the therapist and the client remains confidential.

In NLP, there is the belief in the need for the perfection of the nature of human creation, so every client is encouraged to recognize the sensitivity of the senses and make use of them in responding to specific problems. As a matter of fact, NLP also holds the belief that it is possible for the mind to find cures to diseases and sicknesses.

The techniques employed by NLP have to do with a noninvasive, medicine-free therapy that enables the client to find out new ways of handling emotional issues such as low self-esteem, lack of confidence, anxiety, and destructive relationship patterns. It is also a successful tool in effective bereavement counseling.

With its roots in the field of behavioral science, which was developed by Skinner, Pavlov, and Thorndike, NLP makes use of the combination of physiology and the unconscious mind to bring about change in the thought process and ultimately the behavior of a person.

NLP Techniques

Here are some of the techniques that are employed in the users of NLP:

Dissociation

Everyone experience a bad day when a situation ruins it and gives one a bad feeling. This may drown your spirit every time you are faced with it. Also, it may be a certain nervous feeling that comes at any point that you have to address an audience. It could be a feeling of shyness whenever you need to approach a certain (special) person.

Although it may seem as this feeling of shyness, sadness or nervousness is automatic and unstoppable, what the NLP technique of dissociation offers are ways to get over these feelings.

Get to know about the emotion that you wish to overcome especially when feeling discomfort, anger, or dislike for a certain situation.

Imagine the possibility of teleportation and looking back at yourself going through the same situation, but this time from an observer's point of view. Take note of the dramatic change that occurs in the feelings.

To get an extra boost for your morale, think about floating out of your body and watching yourself. This means that you will now be looking at yourself while your other self is also looking at yourself. What this double dissociation attempts to do is to take away all the negative emotions in all possible minor situations.

Content Reframing

This technique is useful for all the times you feel like you are trapped in a negative or helpless situation. With the help of reframing, you will be able to get rid of all negative situations by becoming empowered by interpreting the meaning of the situation into becoming a positive thing. Take a situation where your relationship ended, for instance. Although it may seem as if it is an awful situation when one looks at it on the surface, what about the possibility of those hidden benefits of being single? Think of the fact that you are now open to meeting and interacting with new people, which means that it is possible for you to get into a new relationship. This means that you are now free to do whatever you want to do at whatever time you want to do it. From the last relationship that ended, you must have learned some valuable lessons that will eventually be useful to you in your subsequent relationship(s). It is very possible to panic or get thrown into fear in certain situations. Instead of focusing on fear, you can sway your focus by reframing. This will contribute to helping you make some even- handed and responsible decisions.

Anchoring Yourself

This process of creating a neurological connection between the ringing of a bell and the attitude of salivating is known as a conditioned response. These responses to stimulus anchors can also be used on humans.

The result of anchoring oneself is that a person gets to link a desired positive emotional response with a specific sensation or a phrase. When you can select a positive emotion or a thought and intentionally link it to a gesture, you will be able to trigger the anchor at every point you feel low, so you will be able to change your feelings immediately. Here are some ways of anchoring yourself:

Take note of the feelings you want to experience. It could be a feeling of happiness, confidence, calmness, etc. Decide on the part of your body where you would love to place the anchor. This could be a certain action like pulling your earlobe, squeezing your fingernail, or touching your knuckle. With this physical touch, you will be able to trigger the desired positive feeling whenever you want to. This has nothing to do with the part of the body that you have chosen, all that needs to be done is create that connection between the unique touch and the feelings. You do not have to make this touch for anything else besides the feeling. Think about a certain time in the past when you had the same feelings you are experiencing at a given moment. Reminisce on the time you felt the same way then float into your body by looking through your eyes so that you will be able to replay and relive the memory.

Once done, you can make some adjustments to your body language to match with the memory and the state of mind. When you are reliving the memory, make sure you can see, hear, and feel everything the way you remember it. If you can do this, the feeling will come back, just as it will when you tell a funny story from the past to your friend.

Generalizations

A generalization, like most other things, can have a positive or a negative impact. On the positive side, some generalizations help you organize information in your mind map. For example, when you are a child you begin learning simple words like cup, ball, and dog. If you learn a word like "knob" you also learn that there are doorknobs and volume knobs on the radio, knobs to turn on the lights and knobs on top of pot lids. You generalize "knob" to encompass all knobs.

On the negative side, you can organize information in a way that inhibits and limits your experience in the world and can inaccurately assume certain things about yourself and others. You may have an uncomfortable confrontation with a member of a certain religious background, and you then generalize all people of that religion to be confrontational. You may have a bad experience in a relationship with a woman, and then generally believe a certain thing about all women and dating.

Universal Quantifiers

This language asks, "Always? Never? Everyone?

Since generalizations take a few instances to represent a whole group, there have to be no exceptions to the details of the information in the way that they are organized. They have to fit into the general idea. Generalization categorizes information so that it can be more easily understood since we perceive massive amounts of information daily.

In order to properly categorize our experience, we will sometimes use universal quantifiers to remove any possible exception to our generalization. These quantifiers appear as words like "all," "every," "always," "never," and "none."

Some examples of universal quantifier statements are:

- I never enjoy my time at the museum.

- I always walk this route.

- It's all or nothing.

- Every time this happens, I get a headache.

- None of these products looks okay to me.

You can also make generalizations with universal quantifiers without using these specific words:

- Chinese food tastes bad.

- Owning a home is too expensive.

- Poets are insufferable.

- Dogs are better than cats.

- Politicians are liars.

In order to expose and alter this kind of language, you have to ask the question, "Has there ever been a time when…?"

- Has there ever been a time when Chinese food did taste good to you?

- Has there ever been a time when you enjoyed a poetry reading?

- Has there ever been a time when you did enjoy your time at the museum?

Using this type of question gives you or someone else in your life an opportunity to rethink and reframe their statement. There may have been a time, in which case generalizing that all Chinese food is bad is inaccurate.

Sometimes, the answer to the question "Has there ever ben a time…?" is No. If someone answers no to that question, then you can reframe the experience by asking, "Do you actually like Chinese food? Do you think that it all tastes terrible to you because you don't like it, or because you think it's all bad and that no one else could?"

Generalizing is limiting. Your unique experience of life doesn't have to be limited. Much of it comes down to knowing how language impacts your reality, and how questioning your thought patterns is an effective tool for coming into better alignment with what you want, not what can never happen or always fails.

Learn from The Masters
Of NLP

Powerful Wisdom, Condensed

By this point in the book you have a detailed understanding of not only the theory and framework behind Dark NLP but also how to apply the techniques to get what you want and need

out of life. One of the key concepts of Dark NLP is not learning how to do something through trial and error, but instead seeking out someone who has already made the mistakes for you and following their footsteps to success.

With this principle of seeking out the greatness in mind, you will now be given three insights into the various ways that ideas from NLP can be applied. The three people who have been chosen for this chapter show the various uses for NLP. They all share a common ability to take the principles and techniques of NLP and use them in a certain area of life in a way that is able to capture the imagination of the public at the same time.

For each of the three figures, you will be given some key insights into exactly what has led their understanding of NLP to become so influential within their chosen field. You will have the key concepts they teach distilled and summarized in a way that makes them easy to grasp. In addition to factual information about the people and what they teach, you will be given a succinct summary of the main ways they can be modeled. Their outlooks in life, and the ways they can be applied for your benefit, will be carefully detailed.

Ross Jeffries

Ross Jeffries is one of the most notorious and divisive names within the world of NLP. He is infamous for taking the concepts of NLP and applying them to the world of seduction. Jeffries is said to be the basis for various Hollywood characters exhibiting behaviors of this cocky, self-assured guru. Jeffries is loathed by many for using shock value marketing techniques to draw negative attention to NLP. He is considered by some to condone unacceptable ideas such as not taking into account the level of consent and permission that is present in an interaction.

Jeffries is also known for having a series of high-profile disagreements and feuds with former students. A common theme to these controversies is Jeffries feeling as if he has somehow been unfairly treated. In the landmark book of seduction The Game, author Neil Strauss detailed how Jeffries was bitter whenever another teacher disagreed with his understanding of seduction.

Ross Jeffries has featured in a number of high profile television documentaries. In these, he has been able to showcase the power of his applications of NLP, including his ability to seductively anchor deeply powerful positive feelings to himself in a short space of time.

Their Unique Take

Perhaps the key contribution of Ross Jeffries to the world of NLP is his ability to take the principles and techniques in general and refine them for a specific purpose. While many users of NLP had long been aware of their potential to enhance romantic interactions, Jeffries was the first to formalize a system. In doing so, Jeffries paved the way for many later teachers who would adapt the concepts of NLP into their own formal method of study.

Jeffries was also one of the first high profile NLP teachers to tap into the potential of marketing NLP in a way which suggests it almost gives its users superpowers. Jeffries was able to suggest that taking one of his seminars or buying one of his products would enable the purchaser to exercise a godlike level of control over other people. While it is true that NLP does greatly enhance the levels of influence a person experiences, Jeffries made it sound like something unimaginably profound.

One of the legacies of Jeffries within the world of NLP is his contribution to the use of in-depth, technical jargon to refer to different concepts. He uses a variety of unique words to describe everyday activities. For example, meeting members of the opposite sex is known as 'sarging.' Ironically, Jeffries use of this type of language is an example of NLP concepts being used against its own customers. Jeffries is fostering a sense of 'Us vs. Them' in which the chosen insiders understand the secret language that is spoken. In order to continue this positive feeling of being on the inside, people are willing to continue spending money on products and seminars.

The Lessons

The lessons that can be learned from Ross Jeffries mainly revolve around the power of applying NLP in a concentrated area of life. In the case of Jeffries, he showed that existing techniques could be modified and used to seduce people. You can take this idea of modified application and apply it to almost any area. For example, imagine you work in sales. You can ask yourself questions such as "How can this technique be used to help close a sale? "and "How do the ideas behind NLP relate to the ideas behind sales?" By seeking commonalities between NLP and a specific area of life you will devise unique and effective applications of its concepts.

We can also learn from Jeffries the importance of expressing our ideas in a memorable and attention-grabbing way. The genius of Jeffries was not in inventing new ideas - it was presenting existing ideas in a way that was understandable and easy to remember. When we are trying to explain our ideas to someone we should be sure to summarize them and use techniques such as alliteration and emotional language to increase the chances of being recalled later. If you are able to come across as charismatic then you are more likely to have your words remembered.

Tony Robbins

Tony Robbins is one of the most well-known and recognizable teachers of motivation and self-improvement techniques in the world. He is known for his series of books, audio products and seminars which help people to take control of their lives and find ways to tap into their states of peak performance and creativity.

Ever since Tony Robbins' earliest book, he has made direct reference to the power of NLP to achieve rapid results. Robbins is an advocate of NLP to help people realize what they want out of life, motivate themselves to take action and to stay motivated along their journey. Robbins draws upon both the broad concepts underpinning NLP, as well as specific techniques found within it, to help people unlock their potential in life.

Their Unique Take

Robbins' unique take on NLP was the ability to combine it with other related concepts to enhance its power and appeal. For example, Robbins was able to combine ideas such as NLP visualizations with methods drawn from literature related to time management and goal setting to give people a system that was more powerful than any of its component parts.

Robbins was also able to directly link the benefits of using NLP with his own techniques and teachings. Often, people are turned off from NLP because the people explaining it focus too heavily on the process itself and the concepts behind it, rather than conveying the benefits a person will experience as a result of using NLP. Robbins was able to convince people to buy into what he was teaching as he sold them on how it would improve their life in the process.

Robbins was also able to build trust in himself and his methods by presenting an impressive track record. No matter which stage of his career Robbins was at, he was able to refer to his past achievements in a way that made his words sound credible. For example, in his earliest book, Robbins was able to talk about using NLP to help a large number of patients overcome their addictions and phobias in a far shorter space of time than traditional therapy would allow. In his next book, Robbins was able to refer to the millions of people helped by his first book, and so forth. No matter how famous Robbins was, he was able to make a positive and convincing example from his past.

Robbins was also one of the most prominent mainstream teachers of using the NLP understanding of values for personal motivation. Robbins made the connection between understanding our values and tying them into our everyday activities to lend them greater meaning and significance. Robbins had observed in his years of practice that people were more inclined to stick with a course of action if they felt it was in harmony with their wider view of the world and what mattered in it. Robbins also had the ability to present NLP as one tool in a wider, holistic approach to self-improvement and management. He presented the teachings of NLP as existing in harmony with other aspects of self improvement such as health and fitness, nutrition and memory retention. In doing this, Robbins was able to make NLP seem more acceptable to a wider number of people. By presenting NLP as one tool of many, rather than the 'one true path', Robbins removed any suspicion of NLP as being dogmatic or somehow cult-like.

The Lessons

A number of lessons can be drawn from the example of Tony Robbins. First, we can use his model to understand how NLP fits in with the other activities in our life. For example, we might hold strong opinions on social policy and the way in which a society should act. How does our understanding of Dark NLP support or challenge these notions? Do we gain a greater insight into another aspect of life through our usage of Dark NLP?

Robbins also teaches people to constantly keep in mind the need to look beyond the apparent meaning of words and events. This is in harmony with the Dark

NLP teaching that it is not the apparent surface meaning of things that matters; instead, it is the personal meaning that people assign to them. This manifests in the Dark NLP practices of always striving to ensure you understand what a person means when they use a given word, and remembering to take everyone as a unique individual, rather than making behavioral assumptions based on the behavior of other people. Robbins also makes clear the need to have both motivation and strategy in order to achieve our aims in life. It is not enough to only feel motivated because motivation is short-lived and will wear off. If all we have is our motivation, then our efforts are likely to be inconsistent and our goals elusive. It is important to combine the temporary ups and downs of motivation with something more substantial - a tried and tested strategy of how to achieve our goals, that has been carefully modeled from someone who has succeeded in similar circumstances to ours. We can also learn from Robbins how NLP can be used to inspire and energize mass audiences at one time. Robbins is known for embedding his seminars with NLP language that is used to excite and enthuse those watching him. NLP is often emphasized as something that can be used to motivate ourselves or a small number of people at once. Robbins helps inspire us to realize that we can use the ideas of NLP to make a difference to large numbers of people at once.

The Power of Persuasion

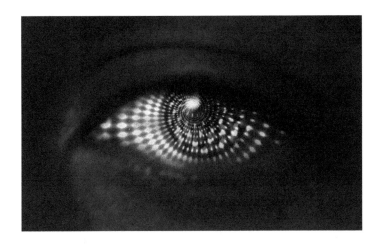

How is it that some people are so good at convincing others to do things? How do some people manage to persuade others into things they wouldn't normally do? The skills of a

manipulator and situation a person is in determine the extent to which one can be influenced. How much can a person persuade you is determined by your current state? For instance, if you are lonely, hungry tired, or even needy in some way, then the chances of you being persuaded rise. Simply put, you can get a hungry man to do anything so long as you promise him a plate of food.

So, ensuring that all your basic needs are met, emotionally and physically can make you less susceptible to con artists who appear to offer solutions to them but as for too much in exchange. Something that seems to meet a certain need in your life, more so if it is basic can seem very persuasive. One might think that he/she will notice when a person is trying to manipulate him or her but, the techniques used to persuade are very subtle, and some of the tools used are very basic thus we are not always conscious of them.

According to psychologist Robert Cialdini, there are six major principles of persuasion, and they are not always used for bad intentions. He explains that if a person used these skills to improve the lives of others, then it is a good thing. If someone persuaded the other not to drink and drive, then that is a good thing.

Factors affecting the power and effect of persuasion, according to Robert Cialdini

Reciprocity

The first and most common principle affecting persuasion is reciprocity. Basically, you will find that whenever a person does you a favor, you feel obligated to do something in return to show appreciation. Interestingly, this feeling is in the subconscious mind such that we are not really aware of its presence. A statement such as "I owe you one" or "I am much obliged" is used to show someone that we are grateful for their assistance and that we can hope in and help them whenever needed because of something they have done for us.

A manipulator who knows these techniques can use a small favor to get to you to reciprocate. Sometimes, this manipulator will look for something that you really need and step in to help. In return, they will ask for something that is way out of your bracket. And because 'you are obliged,' you will reciprocate the favor. The concept of reciprocity has been used widely by companies. First, they offer free samples to customers who will then feel the need to give back by buying the item even if it does not meet the standards.

I noticed that one of my friends does not accept free samples in malls, so I asked her why she does not sample the designer perfumes offered. She said, "That is how we get trapped. You sample it, and they salesperson talk you into buying it even though it is overpriced. And since you already sampled, reciprocity comes into play." That explanation made a lot of sense to me.

Of course, there are people who do favors for others without expecting anything in return, but you have to beware. Others are manipulative, and in the majority of us, the feeling of owing someone is a very big decision influencer.

Self-consistency

Another principle of persuasion is self-consistency. Robert Cialdini found some people are more likely to stick with an idea or goal they committed to (verbally or in writing) because of self-image. There are people who associate commitment with self-image and personality. Though there is nothing wrong with being committed, some extent is not justified. These people who apply the principle of self-consistency can get so lost in their idea that even when it becomes invalid, they continue to honor it.

We like to present a consistent image to the world and to ourselves. As such, it becomes hard to leave a thing we started even after realizing that it is not worthy. Gradually, we develop a sense of sympathy to the idea we have been following such that quitting is hard. The term brainwashing is derived from a Chinese expression that literally means 'to wash the brain.' The concept of brainwashing became clear during the Korean War. The Chinese who were instructed to repeat certain pro-Communist and anti-American ideas to prisoners gradually began to believe the statements themselves. A believe you practiced but did not believe gradually becomes part of you. People who follow the lead bully often start out doing small favors and tasks. After a while, it becomes hard to leave the practice because of maintaining face in public. So, when the lead bully becomes absolutely selfish to others, the followers are unable to make a different choice. Do not underestimate the power of the fear of loneliness. Do not undermine the need to be consistent and to feel. It can make a person do things he/she would not do under normal circumstances.

Social proof

The power of social proof is something no one can deny. We are mostly herd creatures of society in many ways. As human beings, we tend to follow what others are doing. IGF a million people are doing a

certain thing, then they cannot be wrong, so we follow them. Do you think people would wear pants that revealed their innerwear if no one else was doing it? If a large number of people start to sing along some weird songs, chances are, others will join the crowd. We tend to do things done by other people.

Of course, we have to realize that there are things done by crowds with perfectly good reasons. However, there is a 'madness of the crowd' concept whereby we do not want to think for ourselves. That is a very strong persuasion tool used by manipulators and persuaders.

Perceived authority

One powerful persuader is a confident, authoritative attitude. Have you ever walked into an office with nothing but confidence and authority and gotten what you want? Do you understand why they say confidence is very important during an interview? An authoritative manner can persuade people. Anyone will think that you have power and knowledge just because of a confident appearance.

Most of the ex-Nazis explained that they just followed the orders of their leaders. Just because someone with authority said it, then it must be correct. Titles, too, add to the perceived authority. For example, a teacher, a scientist or a king can say anything, and it appears correct.

In the 1960s, Stanley Milgrams did experiments revealing that most people can carry out highly questionable and cruel acts so long as the person asking has the perceived authority. The problem with this [principle of perceived authority is that it can easily be faked by putting on the appropriate uniform, speaking in a certain manner and behaving in a particular way. All of us are capable of falling for fake authority. Once again, we allow someone to do the thinking for us.

Likeability

On the face, there is nothing particularly sinister about likability. Interestingly, it has been identified as the fifth principle of persuasion. Likable people are very persuasive. Everyone can easily fall for the charm of a likable person. It has been found that people are more likely to purchase things from someone they like, and that is why many companies look for likable salespersons. Likable people are often attractive, and if they try too hard, it comes across as smarmy. However, if we truly like them, there are high chances of us purchasing things from them. In fact, how many times have you heard a person who was conned say, "but he/she seemed nice"?

The world has confirmed the concept that attractive people are more likable, cleverer, braver, and better than plain ones. That mentality is termed as 'the Halo effect.' The challenge is, even the most attractive people might not have pure intentions towards you.

Scarcity

The fact that gold is rear makes it more interesting to find and purchase. You have heard people say that if diamonds grew on trees, no one would care about them, but now that they are rear, we value them. What makes them so precious is their scarcity – there are not many of them around. That is why offers in the malls have deadlines. It is also the reason why you hear sales person saying, "We can only give this offer till Monday" or "This offer is valid while this stock lasts, and people are buying a lot." The thought that these items will soon be scarce will make you want to make a purchase. The perceived scarcity adds value to the product.

In the case of people, this scarcity experiences run deep and affect us more than we think. For instance, if we have a partner or spouse who is grumpy moody and disagreeable most of the time, we might fall into the trap of feeling extremely grateful when they display a shred of

happiness. In such a case, we will be manipulated into doing things for the person in order to get a glimpse of that rare happy moment. Their pleasant behavior is scarce and is, therefore, very valuable to us.

Psychologist B.F Skinner, a behavioralist found that inconsistent rewards are more compulsive and addictive because of the scarcity. Therefore, a dog that is not always rewarded with food will act more compulsively than that which is used to food every now and then. Unbelievable but true, if gambling involved sure wins all the time; it would not be as interesting. Maybe the person who keeps going back to the abusive relationship is just addicted to the few good times that occur in that relationship. So, be on the safe side and stay aware of the people using the scarcity principle on you.

Beware of the people using these principles. Do not get persuaded by manipulators just because you are under the influence of scarcity or liking. Do not fall for fake authority or social proof tricks. It is okay to change if you find that something is not working as expected. If need be, lose the self-consistency and need to reciprocate.

Neuro-Linguistic Programming Manipulation Techniques

Visual squash

Visual squash is one of the most popular NLP technique of all time. It assists an individual in the road to acknowledging how each part constitutes a whole. What you should keep in

mind about this particular technique is that every piece is integrated to a level that is relatively higher than what has been previously decided based on what the limits are. This is done until a unified state is achieved. There is also a tendency that this process would pile up until every level of logic that is deemed as the unconscious is attained. Every part is described in relation to its ability to function well and its relationship with its corresponding parts. Nevertheless, experts have commented as to how visual squash is a productive and efficacious tactic in settling conflicts among the different parts. As soon as there is unity among these parts, you will have a high chance of producing success.

The main idea of visual squash is rooted in the process of reconditioning a former emotion or thought into something much more positive. There is a high chance that this former emotion or thought used a negative pattern, which can be seen as an obstacle to achieving your ultimate goal. Thus, the sooner you are able to decondition, the sooner you can recondition, and the sooner you can achieve success. Decondition entails the removal of your old perspective. Recondition, on the other hand, is the act of replacing these old perspectives into positive emotions.

The steps to deconditioning and reconditioning are as follows:

- Visualizing the negative pattern

As the term suggests, visual squash is the act of squashing a particular mental image. This mental image is a negative pattern; so, to squash it, you have to visualize it first. Experts have advised that it would be better to put this negative thought into an animated scenario. You can even exaggerate the negative thought to stress its negativity. For example, you are always late. Your visualization may include you arriving in class only to find that it is already over.

- Visualizing the replacement pattern

After visualizing the negative pattern, try to visualize the replacement pattern. In this step, you try to think of the positive version of the initial pattern. Instead of imagining scenarios wherein you are always late, imagine how you are always on time. Make it visual on your mind and exaggerate every possible detail. You can imagine yourself being the first one to arrive in class.

- Chaining the two states

In this chapter, you have learned how chaining two states work. Now, you will start with the negative pattern at the start and the final pattern, which is a positive pattern, at the end. Usually, it would be up to the individual whether they will provide some middle scenario that would bridge the two patterns. Nevertheless, you have to visualize transitioning from the beginning to the end.

- Deconditioning process

In addition, in this chapter, you learned how to properly decondition and recondition certain scenarios. Moreover, in the process of chaining the two states, you free the initial pattern, which is a negative

pattern, and you visually squash it in your mind. The visual component of this technique is crucial. You must eliminate all details related to the initial pattern so that you can only dwell on those associated with a positive thought.

- Reconditioning process

Finally, you recondition and allow yourself to swell on the new positive pattern. Start to visualize yourself as someone who has a new mindset, someone who has a behavioral pattern that has proven itself useful to you as an individual. With that in mind, you are better able to relate to other people. You will learn that communicating with them is a simple and hassle-free process. Even when you accidentally go back to your negative pattern, your mind will automatically recondition itself into a state that is positive.

Collapsing anchors

Do remember that anchors are defined as either positive or negative. The main point of all of these is to eliminate negative thoughts. In relation to manipulation, you can use this NLP technique to manipulate yourself into getting rid of your bad habits. The same goes for when you want another person to do your bidding.

The entire process is the same. The difference would lie in the thought pattern that you would want the other person to acknowledge or get rid of. Part of this entire process is the collapsing of the negative anchors. As explained, anchors are established by associating to a particular state, and it brings about a certain state that you desire to accomplish at the same time you are attempting to realize its actual success.

On another note, keep in mind that negative anchors have the potential to tamper with your positive state allowing you to feel uncertain about specific things, especially if it has been originally affiliated with a negative experience.

Thus, there is a need for you to learn how to successfully collapse these anchors so that you are better able to remove any association with this negativity. You can do this by following the succeeding steps:

• Identifying the negative anchor

Of course, there is a need for you first to identify the anchor. As explained, an anchor can be a thought, a feeling, or an experience. At first, you will start to recognize more than one anchors; however, you need to be able to narrow the list down only to those negative ones; this will ease the process of collapsing them one by one. As soon as the anchor has been identified, take control of it and try to visualize it as much as you can. For this example, let us imagine the negative anchor of anger.

- Choosing the alternative anchor

Similar to when you are trying to chain two states, you need to be able to identify a replacement or an alternative anchor. For this, let us use the positive anchor of joy.

This will replace your initial negative anchor of anger. In all honesty, you will find that choosing an alternative, something that is the exact opposite of your initial anchor and something that covers every negative association is a lot easier. The positive anchor of joy represents love and humor; this will be a great alternative that would meet all of your emotional needs.

- Linking the alternative anchor

As soon as you select an alternative anchor, proceed to gather information from your mind that is firmly attached to the feeling of joy. When you hear the word joy, what are you reminded of? You can think of a happy memory for when you were still a child.

Probably, a time when you and your mother would visit the park every afternoon. You can even try to bring a more physical state, such as a picture of you and your mother at the park. The trigger is the photo, and you are trying to acknowledge the emotion that is tied to the trigger.

- Collapsing the negative anchor

If possible, you also bring in a physical state of your negative anchor. This object should be something that angers you. You can use this to draw out any negative emotions. If you do not have an external anchor, you can rely on the internal anchors. Visualize the negative anchor and immediately replace it with a more positive one. As soon as you link the two anchors, proceed to collapse the negative anchor. As a result, every time this negative emotion would come to you, connect it to the alternative anchor, and collapse it so that you are only left with the positive anchor.

- Application process

One of the most important process steps in the entirety of NLP techniques is that you can apply it. There is a need to always keep the end in mind. As soon as you visualize the negative thought pattern, immediately link it to a positive one, and collapse the initial state. Some have commented on how having an alternative state that has much more intensity greatly helps in squashing the negative pattern. This process allows you to relinquish any associated anchors. Furthermore, this can easily be applied to a variety of things in the real world. You can use this to eliminate a bad habit or a bad thought. Moreover, you can use this to manipulate people into eliminating any of their bad habit or bad thought. The more you are able to visualize these patterns, the better.

- Step reframing

At some point, you will realize that not all behavioral patterns are perfect. There are those that posit good intentions, but there exists a negative aspect of their behavior. Mastery of NLP techniques states that you must be able to accurately distinguish and point out bad elements, even in the best motives.

Remember when we talked all about Secondary Gain, as well as Julianne's back pain? Well, behind every good or bad behavior, there will always be a positive intent. However, experts have claimed that in an attempt to achieve a positive state, an individual unconsciously undergoes imperfections, which may result in a negative outcome. If there is, one thing to remember about positive intentions is that limitations on a certain standard should be accepted with the bigger picture in mind. Approaching a situation blindly can only bring about disaster. There is a need to recognize all probable effects that a specific choice may have on the situation.

- Identifying the behavior

To successfully perform step reframing, you must first identify a particular behavior in yourself. Even though the intention may appear to be good, you will soon realize that it has underlying symptoms associated with the behavior. These underlying symptoms can be negative aspects of an action, feeling, or thought you once had. In identifying the behavior, you have to be very specific so that you would know the appropriate response for this situation.

- Identifying the part that triggers that particular behavior

After you have identified the behavior, you must search your memory, past experiences, and emotions for a particular aspect that brings about this behavior. It could be a memory or mental picture that tends to flash everyone in a while whenever you would find yourself in a

distressing environment. Try to assess which of these triggers that particular behavior. Try envisioning it clearly in your mind so that you would know which could cause such an adverse behavior.

CONCLUSION

Thank you for reading all this book!

The manipulator plans to know where your weakness is and exploit it, you may even throw the blame game on yourself for not doing It is very imperative to reassure yourself that you are not part of the problem. Remember that you are just being manipulated to feel bad about your actions and surrender your rights and power in the end. You need to consider the kind of relationship you have with the manipulator as well.

As opposed to just doing what is most comfortable and fastest, do not forget about your actions' consequences. Remember that psychological manipulators are the best for making their option the easiest, fastest, and the least hurtful. They are also best at keeping the people focused on their current feelings. That explains why people do things they later regret. Instead of dealing with a consequence, make sure you choose to do something that you won't be forced to rethink.

You have already taken a step towards your improvement.

Best wishes!

.